Tables

EASY WORD ESSENTIALS 2019

BOOK 4

M.L. HUMPHREY

ISBN: 978-1-63744-062-9

SELECT TITLES BY M.L. HUMPHREY

WORD ESSENTIALS 2019

Word 2019 Beginner

Word 2019 Intermediate

EASY WORD ESSENTIALS 2019

Text Formatting

Page Formatting

Lists

Tables

Track Changes

CONTENTS

Introduction

The *Easy Word Essentials 2019* series of books is designed for those users who just want to learn one specific topic rather than have a more general introduction to Microsoft Word 2019, which is provided in *Word 2019 Beginner* and *Word 2019 Intermediate*.

Each book in this series covers one specific topic such as formatting, tables, or track changes.

I'm going to assume in these books that you have a basic understanding of Microsoft Word. However, this book does include an appendix with basic terminology just in case I use a term that isn't familiar to you or that isn't used the way you're used to.

This entire series of books is written for users of Word 2019. If you have a different version of Word then you might want to read the *Easy Word Essentials* series instead which is written as a more general approach to learning Microsoft Word.

For most introductory topics there won't be much of a difference between the two, but just be aware that this particular series does not worry about compatibility with other versions of Word whereas the more general series does.

Also, just a reminder that the content of this book is directly pulled from *Word 2019 Beginner* and/or *Word 2019 Intermediate* so there may be references in the text that indicate that.

Alright. Now that the preliminaries are out of the way, let's dive in with a discussion of tables.

Tables Overview

Tables are incredibly useful for presenting a summary of information. I used these all the time in my corporate career. (Not so much in English class.)

A table is essentially a grid of spaces composed of x number of columns and y number of rows. Once you create that grid any text you enter into one of the spaces is contained within that space.

I find tables are the easiest way to control exactly where text that isn't in simple paragraphs appears on the page.

They also are the easiest way to use formatting with that type of text. For example, the first row of almost any table I've ever used I've shaded it a different color from the rest of the rows in my table. I could do that outside of a table, but it works better with a table.

Insert

Let's dive in, starting with how to insert a basic table into your document.

You do so by going to the Tables section of the Insert tab and clicking on the dropdown arrow under Table.

There you will see a grid of squares under the heading Insert Table as well as options below that for Insert Table, Draw Table, Excel Spreadsheet, and Quick Tables.

If you had text in your document that you selected before clicking on the dropdown, you'd also see an option for Convert Text to Table.

Let's start with the Insert Table set of squares at the top of the dropdown menu.

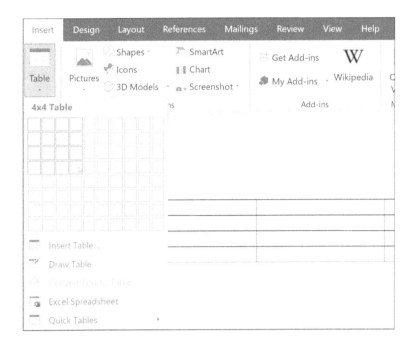

To insert a table using this option, simply hold your mouse over the square that would be in the bottom right corner of the table you want to start with. So above I've put my cursor over the fourth square from the right and fourth square from the top to create a 4x4 table.

As you move your mouse around over the squares you'll see that a table appears within your document with that number of rows and columns.

The title "Insert Table" in the dropdown also changes to reflect the dimensions of the table you're about to insert. Which is why in the image above it says 4x4 Table above the selected squares in the dropdown..

By default, all columns are of an equal width to cover the width of the page or the width of the space you're working in if that happens to be smaller. (For example, you can create a table and then insert another table within a space of that table and the columns in your second table will have a width determined by the size of that space not the whole page.)

Rows are of a standard height that's driven by the current font size in your document.

Unless you're pasting in data, the number of rows is probably not that important. But do try to get the right number of columns initially because they're harder to add later. (The number of columns can be adjusted it's just not quite as easily as adjusting the number of rows.)

To actually insert your table, click on the square.

Your next option for inserting a table is to use the Insert Table option below those squares. When you click on that it will open the Insert Table dialogue box where you can type in the number of rows and columns that you want in your table. Just click into each box and type the number you need, or use the arrows on the sides to increase or decrease the number for rows and columns.

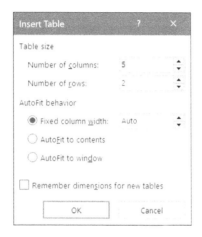

In the AutoFit Behavior section below that, if you use the arrows next to Auto for the Fixed Column Width value you can specify an exact width to use for each column rather than letting the columns fill the page or space you're working in.

Click OK or hit enter when you're done and Word will insert the table into your document.

The Draw Table option is one I don't use. It lets you click on your document and drag to draw a large square that is the overall size of your table and then you can click and drag again to draw the lines for columns and rows. This is probably the best option for a table where the number of columns or the number of rows are not going to stay consistent, like in this table here:

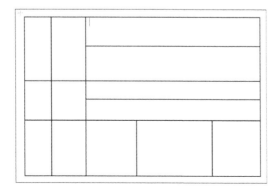

You can get the same effect using split or merge cells, but this was a much quicker and easier option. I just generally don't need a table like the one above.

The final option in the dropdown is Quick Tables. If you scroll past the calendar options there are some basic formatted tables you can use:

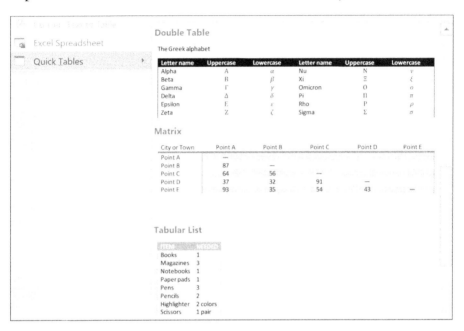

They insert exactly as you see them, text and all, so if you use one you'll need to overwrite that text with your own values. (Personally, I'd rather format a new table myself, but if any of those options have a base-level appearance you like it could be a time saver to use one.)

The Excel spreadsheet option will embed an Excel spreadsheet in your document. It initially opens as an Excel rectangle within the document where you can enter values. Once you are done doing so, hit Esc, and it will appear as a basic table in your document. Double-clicking on that table will then open it as an Excel file that can be edited. (Although on my computer it froze and wouldn't open.)

I have used this option in PowerPoint in the past, but I find it to be generally finicky so I tend to avoid it when I can. (You can just as easily create your table and then copy and paste in your data from Excel. Granted, that means the two files aren't connected, but hopefully your Word document is just a summary document anyway.)

Okay, so those are the ways to insert tables. Now let's talk about how to add information and change the structure of your table after the fact.

Contents

Adding Content

To add contents to a table, you can simply click into the table and start typing. Use the Tab key to move to the next cell to the right. If you're at the end of the row it will move you to the first cell in the next row. If you're at the end of the table, Tab from the last cell will create a new row that is added to the end of the table.

Shift + Tab will move one cell to the left. If you're at the beginning of a row it will move up a row to the last cell in the prior row.

Enter creates a line break within a cell. It will not move you down to the next cell in your table. You can, however, use the up and down arrows to move up or down a row in your table and the right and left arrows to move to the next cell to the right or left in a table.

If you enter text that takes up more space than is currently available in that row, the height of the row will increase to keep all of your text visible.

Word 2019 also may by default expand the width of your columns to accommodate the text you enter into a column so that the text all stays on one line. (Once you change this setting it appears to stay changed, however.)

If you want to adjust this setting, you can right-click on the table and choose Table Properties from the dropdown menu to open the Table Properties dialogue box. Next, go to the Table tab and click on Options. From there either check or uncheck "Automatically Resize to Fit Contents".

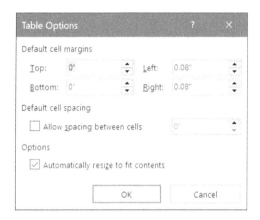

Your other option is to click on the table and go to the Table Tools Layout tab which should appear as a menu tab.

Click on the dropdown for AutoFit in the Cell Size section and choose Fixed Column Width or AutoFit Contents from the dropdown.

If the information you want to put into your table already exists elsewhere, for example, an Excel spreadsheet, you can copy it from the other location and paste it (Ctrl + V) into your Word document.

To do so, you need to select in your table the same number of rows and columns that exist in your source document. So if you're pasting a 5 cell by 2 cell set of data from Excel, you should select five columns and two rows in your table before you paste.

If you don't do this and instead click into a cell in your table and paste, all of the data will paste into just that one cell.

If you don't select a big enough area to paste into then only the data that matches the area you did select will paste.

Select too many cells and the data will start repeating itself to fill the selected number of cells.

Deleting Content

To delete the contents of a table, you can select all of the cells in the table and then use the Delete key. The table will remain, but all of the text will be removed. If the table is set to AutoFit, when you do this the width of the table may shrink considerably since each column will be only one character wide at that point.

You can also delete the contents in a single cell by clicking into that cell and using the delete or backspace keys. Delete if you're on the left-hand side of what you want to remove, backspace is you're on the right-hand side.

Using the backspace key after selecting the entire table will delete the table as well as its contents.

Using the backspace key with a subset of cells in the table will delete those cells from the table. (More on that in the next section where we talk about how deleting cells works in a table.)

Structure

Once you've inserted a table into your document and started putting some text in the cells, chances are you'll want to adjust the format of your table. Maybe you want to widen a column or a row or add one or delete one.

There are many, many options for doing so. Let's walk through some of them.

Column Width

There are a number of ways to adjust the width of a column in a table.

First, you can place your cursor over the line between two columns. Your cursor should turn into something that looks like two parallel lines with arrows pointing to the left and the right. (You'll probably only be able to see the arrows since the parallel lines will be lined up with the line separating the two columns.)

Once your cursor looks like this, you can left-click on the line between the two columns and drag the line to the left or the right to change the width of the column. This will change the width of both columns at once. The total space taken up by both columns remains fixed.

You can also click and drag the line at either end of the table. (In other words, the left-hand side of the first column or the right-hand side of the last column.) In that case, only the width of that first or last column will change, but the overall width of the table will also change.

The second option is to right-click into a cell in the column you want to change and choose Table Properties from the dropdown menu. This will bring up the Table Properties dialogue box. From there go to the Column tab and change your preferred width by entering an exact width in inches.

You can also change the dropdown there from inches to percent and then enter a number between 1 and 100 that represents the percent of the table width that column should take up. So, for example, 50 would make that column 50 percent of the total table width.

If there's already text in the table this may behave a little strangely because it's not going to hide existing text. You can't have a column that is 99 percent of the table width if the other columns have enough text to take up more than 1 percent of the width of the table.

Also, it will never actually set any column to be 100 percent even if you tell it to if there are other columns in the table.

You can change the width of all columns at once to be the same width using this approach by selecting the whole table or an entire row in the table first and then adjusting the value for column width in the dialogue box.

An easy way to select the whole table is by clicking on the box with four arrows in the top left corner of the table. It should appear as soon as you put your mouse over the table.

Your third option is to click into the table so that the Table Tools Layout tab appears in the menu section up top and then go to the Cell Size section and change the value there for column width. (It's the second one.)

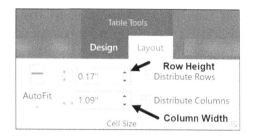

To return to having equally-sized columns you can click on the Distribute Columns option to the right of that input box.

Finally, if you have text that you've entered into a cell, you can have Word AutoFit the width of the cell to the text you've entered by going to the Table Tools Layout tab and clicking on the dropdown arrow under AutoFit in the Cell Size section. From there choose AutoFit Contents.

(Be careful if you do this and only have text in one cell, because all of your other columns will also be adjusted, but to the smallest possible width of just one character wide.)

Row Height

Your options for adjusting the height of a row in your table are mostly the same as for changing the column width, although there will be some row heights you can't achieve because Word forces a minimum row height based upon font size.

First, you can place your cursor over the line dividing any rows in the table and left-click and drag to your desired height. With rows adjusting the height of a row this way WILL NOT adjust the height of any other row.

This does mean that if you adjust the height on any row in the table it will also change the overall height of the table.

Second, you can right-click on any cell in a row and choose Table Properties to bring up the Table Properties dialogue box. From there go to the Row tab and input your desired row height. Your choices are at least or exactly for the value you enter.

(Here is also where you can choose whether or not to let a row break across a page. If you allow this, part of the cell may be on one page and the remainder on another. For rows with a lot of text in them, this may be a necessity.)

Third, you can use the Table Tools Layout tab to specify the row height by changing the number for Height in the Cell Size section. If you want to keep the height of your table as is but make all of your rows the same height, you can click on Distribute Rows.

(AutoFit is not an option for row height. It only works on column width.)

Whichever method you use, be sure to look at the table after you're done, because if you tried to specify a row height that was smaller than Word allows for that font size, it won't have changed.

Table Width

Another attribute of tables that I often change is the overall width of the table.

To do this, right-click on the table and select Table Properties. When the Table Properties dialogue box comes up, go to the Table tab and click on the box for Preferred Width under Size and then specify the width you want for the table in inches.

You can also specify here that your table be X percent of the width of the active area of your document.

Another option is to go to the right-hand side of the table, hover your mouse over that outside column line until you see the two parallel lines with arrows on either side, and then left-click and drag until you have the table width you want.

The problem with this option is that you're basically changing the table size by resizing the last column so it has its limits. If you want to shrink a table, you can only go as far as the minimum width of that last column and then you have to readjust all of the column widths.

Another option if you want the table to be the width of the page is to use AutoFit. Click on the table, go to the Cell Size section of the Table Tools Layout tab, click on the dropdown arrow under AutoFit, and choose AutoFit Window.

Insert a Cell, Row, or Column

If you need to add a cell, row, or column to your table there are a number of ways to do so. We're going to talk about them together because they overlap a great deal.

To insert a cell, click into an existing cell in the table that is where you want to insert the cell. Right-click and on the dropdown menu hold your mouse over the Insert option and then choose Insert Cells from the bottom of new dropdown menu that should appear.

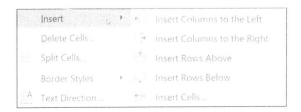

This will open the Insert Cells dialogue box. Your choices are to shift cells right, shift cells down, insert entire row, or insert entire column.

When I choose to shift cells down, Word inserts an entire new row, so that's not an actual option. (But it does make sense that it works that way so that you don't end up with a table with an uneven number of cells in any given row.) So the only real option there for inserting a single cell is to shift cells right.

Now, if you selected a single cell in a single row and inserted a cell doing so would create a table with one cell by itself in its own column at the far end of that row, which is not something I've ever wanted. Generally when working with tables I want to insert an entire row or an entire column.

As you can see with the Insert Cells dialogue box above, those are both also available choices. But you don't actually have to go that far, because (as you can see in the image above that) the Insert dropdown menu also has options for inserting rows and columns.

So you can right-click on your cell, go to Insert, and then choose from the secondary dropdown menu to insert a column to the left or the right of the cell you're clicked into or a row above or below that cell. (The Insert Cells dialogue box option defaults to inserting a row above and a column to the left.)

It is possible to insert more than one cell, row, or column at a time.

If you have a table with five columns in it and want five more columns, the easiest way to do that is to select all five columns and then choose to insert columns to the left or right. Word will insert as many additional columns as you have selected.

Same with rows. Select cells in three rows and choose to insert rows and you'll get three more rows. (And cells, too. Select five cells, you insert five more.)

If you just need a row inserted at the bottom of your table, the easiest way is to use the tab key from the last cell in the table.

(That's why I don't worry so much if I'm building a table where I'm going to input the information manually how many rows there are, because I know that as I reach the last row of the table I can just keep going using the tab key and Word will add the rows for me as I need them.)

Another option you have for inserting rows or columns is located in the Table Tools Layout tab.

Click into the cell in your table where you want to insert and then go to the Rows & Columns section where you have four choices, Insert Above, Insert Below, Insert Left, and Insert Right.

If you hold your mouse over each option it will actually spell out for you that the first two options are for inserting rows and the second two are for columns.

You can click on any of those options to insert a row or column as the case may be. Clicking on the expansion arrow for that section brings up the Insert Cells dialogue box.

(Just a quick note here. If you have your version of Word minimized you may not see the options side-by-side like they are in the image above. When I shrink Word to take up less of my screen the Insert Above option stays where it is but the other three options are listed in one column stacked on top of each other. Just something to be aware of if your display doesn't look quite like mine at any point. The menu adjusts dynamically based on the amount of available space.)

Delete a Cell, Row, or Column

To delete a cell, click on it, right-click, and choose Delete Cells from the dropdown menu. This will bring up the Delete Cells dialogue box where your choices are Shift Cells Left, Shift Cells Up, Delete Entire Row, or Delete Entire Column.

Shift Cells Left will delete the cell as well as its contents. All of the cells in that row to the right of the deleted cell will shift over to fill the empty space. They will keep their contents as well as their original width. The final column of the table will no longer have a cell in it for that row.

(It's not something I'd recommend doing. This works in Excel, but really doesn't in Word.)

Shift Cells Up will delete the content of the cell and will also move the contents of all of the cells in that column that are below that cell up one row,. The number of cells in the table will remain the same, so the cell itself is not actually deleted.

Again, not something I'd necessarily recommend doing, although I have often deleted an entire row or column, so let's cover that now.

To delete a row, you can right-click on any cell in that row and choose Delete Cells and then choose the Delete Entire Row option from the Delete Cells dialogue box.

You can also select at least two of the cells in that row and then use the Backspace key. This will also bring up the Delete Cells dialogue box and allow you to choose Delete Entire Row.

To delete a column works much the same.

You can right-click on a cell in the column you want to delete and choose Delete Cells and then Delete Entire Column from the Delete Cells dialogue box.

Or you can select at least two of the cells in the column you want to delete and use the Backspace key which will bring up the Delete Cells dialogue box where you can select Delete Entire Column.

If you select all of the cells in a column and use the backspace key Word will automatically delete the column without ever bringing up the Delete Cells dialogue box.

If you select all of the cells in a row and then use the Delete Cells dialogue box to Delete Entire Column, that will delete your entire table.

Your final option for deleting cells, columns, and rows is to go to the Table Tools Layout tab, click on the arrow under Delete in the Rows & Columns section and choose Delete Cells, Delete Columns, or Delete Rows from the dropdown. Both Delete Columns and Delete Rows will immediately delete the column(s) or row(s) you have selected. Delete Cells will bring up the Delete Cells dialogue box.

Delete an Entire Table

That Delete dropdown in the Table Tools Layout tab also has a delete table option. But usually what I do is select the whole table by clicking in the top left corner on the box with arrows in it and then Backspace.

You can also select the whole table, right-click, and choose Delete Table from the dropdown menu.

As mentioned above, selecting a table and using Delete will remove the contents of a table but keep the table within your document.

Split or Merge Cells

Above we discussed the Draw Table option for building a table and I mentioned that it was probably the best way to create a table where you want a different number of cells in one row compared to others but that there were other ways to create that same effect by splitting and merging cells.

Splitting a cell lets you take a single cell (or more if you select more) and split it into multiple cells. Merging cells lets you take more than one cell and merge them together to form a single cell.

So, for example, I might have a header I put on a table that uses the first row of that table and merges all of the cells in that row into one single cell.

Like this:

Summary of Quarterly Performance		
Quarter	Good/Bad/Ugly	Comments
Q1	Good	Nice start to the year
Q2	Ugly	That didn't go well

In my opinion, merging the cells in the top row is the easier way to build this table, but I could have also started with a table with one column and split the cells below the first row.

So how do you do this?

To merge cells, select the cells you want to merge, right-click and choose Merge Cells from the dropdown menu.

You can merge across rows and/or columns, so you can merge a set of cells that span two columns and three cells for example.

Unlike in Excel, the text of the cells you merge will remain within your new cell. (In Excel when you do this only the text in the top leftmost cell is kept. In Word all of the text is kept, each cell entry on its own line.)

Another way to merge cells is to select your cells and then go to the Table Tools Layout tab and choose Merge Cells from the Merge section.

Splitting cells works a little differently. You can split a single cell by clicking into it, right-clicking, and choosing Split Cells from the dropdown menu. But that option is only available when you select a single cell in your table. You can't use it if you want to split four cells at once.

If your goal is to split multiple cells (like in the table above if I decided I wanted another column next to Good/Bad/Ugly but wanted to keep everything else sized the way it is), then you need to use the Split Cells option in the Merge section of the Table Tools Layout tab. Select the cells you want to split and then click on Split Cells.

Either approach brings up the Split Cells dialogue box which lets you decide how many rows and columns to split your selection into.

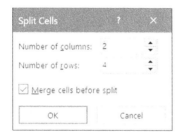

In the example I just mentioned where I want a new set of cells next to the Good/Bad/Ugly column, I would select the cells in that column starting with the header row and then in the Split Cells dialogue box specify the number of rows and columns I want.

The dialogue box will by default show the number of rows in your selection and twice the number of columns, so in this case there would be nothing to change with respect to those values.

However, since my existing cells have text in them, I would need to uncheck the Merge Cells Before Split option before I chose OK.

If you let Word merge the cells before it splits them all of the cell contents will end up split across the cells in your topmost row.

That's how to split cells. They remain part of the same original table, there are just more of them when you're done.

Split a Table

You also have the option to split a table, but when you split a table this creates two separate tables.

I've used this sometimes when manually creating a table of contents in Word that covered more than one page, because it was the easiest way for me to position the table on the second page where I wanted it.

(I know, manual table of contents...Sometimes I don't follow my own best practices. Or am too lazy to add headers throughout a document to enable an automated table of contents.)

So. To split a table, select a cell in the row that you want to be the first row in the second table, go to the Table Tools Layout tab, and click on Split Table in the Merge section.

Word will insert a blank line above that row and you will now have two separate and distinct tables in your document Any adjustments you make to one table, like changing a column width, will not be reflected in the other table.

Repeat A Row At The Top Of Each Page

If you have a table that stretches across multiple pages, chances are you will want to repeat the header row at the top of each page so people know what they're seeing.

Do not do this manually because one little edit and your whole document will be messed up. (Or if you have to change the header row later, you'll need to do so on every, single, page. Ugh. That's a lot of wasted time.)

To tell Word to repeat a row or rows at the top of each page, select at least one cell of each of the rows you want to repeat, go to the Data section of the Table Tools Layout tab, and click on Repeat Header Rows.

The rows you choose to repeat have to be at the top of your table. You can repeat multiple rows, but you can't choose to repeat the second row if you aren't also going to repeat the first row. (The option won't be available.)

Another way to specify that a row needs to repeat on each page is to click into a cell in the row you want to repeat, right-click, choose Table Properties, go to the Row tab of the Table Properties dialogue box, and click on Repeat As Header Row At The Top Of Each Page.

You can do this for multiple rows at once, by selecting one cell from each row before you right-click.

To turn off repeating rows, select a cells in that row(s), go back to the same option and click on it again.

If you have multiple repeating rows, the Table Properties dialogue box will only let you turn them all off at once. The Table Tools Layout tab will let you turn them off individually but it still enforces the rule that you can't repeat the second row if you aren't also repeating the first row and can't repeat the third if you aren't repeating the first and second, etc.

Move

If you have a table that isn't the entire width of the page, chances are you'll need to move it to where you want it on that line. To do this, place your cursor over the table. You should now see a square box appear at the top left corner of the table. It will have arrows pointing in all four cardinal directions.

Left-click on that box and drag the table to where you want it. (This also works for dragging the table to another location in the document.)

If you want to move the table to a different document or a significantly different location in your current document, you can also click on that box in the top left corner, and then Copy (Ctrl + C) or Cut (Ctrl + X) the table, go to the new location, and Paste (Ctrl + V). (The dropdown and Home tab options for copy, cut, and paste will also work.).

The alignment options in the Paragraph section of the Home tab will also work on a table. Just select the table and then click on the alignment option you want (right, left, center). I often use Ctrl + E to center a table as well.

Format

Alright. That's how to structure your table, but what about the aesthetics of the table?

Up above in the Draw a Table example you saw an example of a basic table with simple black lines which is pretty much how all tables will look at the start. In the Split or Merge Cells section I showed you a slightly fancier option where I had bolded and centered text as well as shaded cells. But there's far more than that that you can do with a table.

Let's walk through those options now.

Table Styles

We'll start with the easiest option, which is Table Styles. These are the pre-formatted options that Word gives you. They can be found in the Table Tools Design tab as you can see below where we have the Table Styles section of the Design tab as well as two tables below that with different styles applied to them.

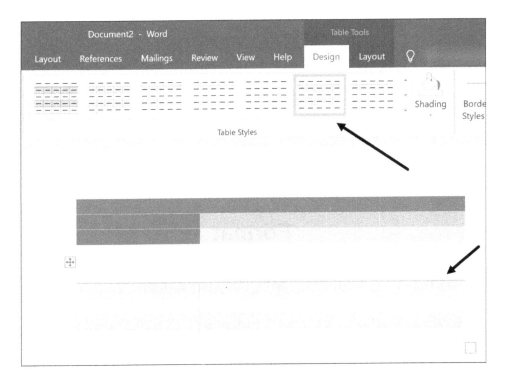

The first style is for a table that has a header row as well as a first column that is also meant to be a label of some sort. The actual rows of data within the table are banded in alternating colors. The second style is much simpler. It just has banded rows but no special formatting for the first row or any of the columns.

You can see what the available styles will look like by clicking on your table and then going to the Table Styles section and holding your cursor over each style. Your table should briefly change to show what the style will look like applied to that table.

To actually apply a style, click on it.

There are more tables than are visible. You can see them by using the up and down arrows to the right-hand side of the visible tables. Clicking on the More arrow just under those options will expand that list of styles to show more at one time and to show their categories: Plain Tables, Grid Tables, and List Tables.

You can then use the scroll bar to see all of the available table styles. I count a total of 105 different Table Style choices.

Clicking on the More option also lets you choose Modify Table Style, Clear, or New Table Style at the bottom.

Be careful of Clear because it erases all lines and special formatting. Your table will still be there so your text will still be separated into cells in that table, but the table itself won't be visible at all. If that's what you want, perfect. Otherwise, avoid this option.

Modify Table Style will open a Modify Style dialogue box where you can change any of the settings on the table style you currently have applied to your table and then overwrite that existing style.

In that dialogue box you can also change the style name and save it as a new style. (If there's a style that's close to what you want this is an easy way to create a style that is exactly what you want, because New Table Style will let you create a brand new style but the base style it's working from is the style with plain black lines and nothing else.)

If you're going to work with table styles begin with the style and then customize from there, because applying a style will often overwrite other formatting.

Table Style Options

In addition to the table styles, there are also six checkboxes to the left of the table styles in a section called Table Style Options. These checkboxes allow you to indicate whether your table should have a header row, total row, banded rows or columns or special formatting for the first column or last column.

From what I can tell they only impact the table appearance when the current table style contains that attribute and you want to remove it. In that case, uncheck the box for the attribute you want to remove from your table.

Shading (Background Fill)

On the right-hand side of the Table Styles section in the Table Tools Design tab is a dropdown for Shading. This is how you fill a cell with background color which is something I often do with header rows in my tables.

To add shading to cells, select the cells where you want to add the shading, go to the Shading dropdown in the Table Tools Design tab, and choose your color. The More Colors option will open the Colors dialogue box which allows you to apply a custom color to your cells using the Custom tab.

Depending on the fill color you choose, you may also need to change the font color in those cells to white so that the text in the cells remains visible.

Another option for adding Shading is to use the Shading option in the Paragraph section of the Home tab. It's also available in the bottom row of the mini formatting menu when you right-click on your table.

There are seventy colors you can choose from in the dropdown and an unlimited number of colors in the Colors dialogue box.

To remove shading, choose the No Color option from the dropdown.

Font, Font Size, Font Color, Etc.

If you want to change the font, font size, text color, add bold or italics to text in a cell, or any other basic text formatting, you can do so in the same way that you would format text in other parts of your document using the Font and Paragraph sections of the Home tab or the mini formatting menu.

For the entire table, click on the box in the top left corner to select all cells in the table first. If it's for specific cells, select those cells. If it's for specific text, select the word(s) you want to format within a cell.

Be careful with changing your font or font size, because the height of the rows in your table will automatically resize to accommodate your text. Depending on your settings, the column widths may change as well.

Table Line Styles, Weight, and Color

Another aspect of a table that you might want to adjust is the appearance of the lines that form the table.

For example, I have manually created a table of contents in the past using a table but didn't want a visible table, so changed the line style to No Border.

I've also had situations where I wanted a thicker outer border around a table and then thinner lines within the table. Also, I've sometimes wanted thicker lines in general (like in the example above for drawing a table where I manually changed each of those lines to a thicker than normal line width to make them more visible.)

To change the lines on a table that you've already created, click on the table and then go to the Borders section of the Table Tools Design tab and choose the line style, weight (thickness), and color you want.

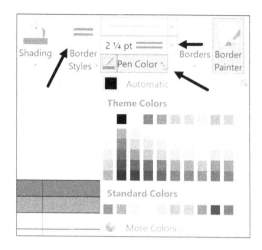

For example, here I've chosen a double border line with a 2 and ¼ pt thickness and a blue color.

At that point, the lines on your table will not have changed. They will remain whatever they were before.

As soon as you make a change to the border style, the Border Painter should turn on. Your cursor will look like a paint brush (If it doesn't, click on Border Painter on the right-hand side of the section.)

To change individual lines to the new line format, simply click on them while the Border Painter is turned on. (Esc will turn it off.)

If you have a large number of lines to change, such as your entire table, use the Borders dropdown menu choices instead which are to the left of the Border Painter option.

In order for this to work, you need to select your entire table first, and then choose your border style. If you just select a cell or click into your table, whatever choice you make will only be applied to that one cell.

For example, if I wanted to apply my new line style to every line in my table, I'd select the entire table and then choose the All Borders option from the Borders dropdown menu.

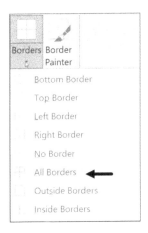

It is possible to use multiple line styles in the same table, but be careful about the order in which you apply them. Depending on what you're trying to do, sometimes it's easier to apply one style as All Borders and then go back through to make refinements on subsections of the table.

I will often do all borders for a plain black line and then apply a thicker border to just the perimeter of the table.

Another option for applying borders or editing the line style of a table is to click on the Expansion arrow from the corner of the Borders section of the Table Tools Design tab or to choose Borders and Shading from the very bottom of the Borders dropdown menu to open the Borders and Shading dialogue box.

The Borders dropdowns in the Paragraph section of the Home tab and the mini formatting menu also will work although you'll need to open the Borders and Shading dialogue box to change the color, weight, and line style.

Using the Border Sampler

If you have a line in a table that is formatted exactly the way you want already, you can sample it and copy its formatting for use on other lines.

To do this, go to the Borders section of the Table Tools Design tab and click on the arrow under Border Styles and then click on the Border Sampler option at the bottom of the dropdown. (You can also right-click on your table, choose Border Styles and then Border Sample from there.)

Your cursor will turn into a little eye dropper. Click on the line with the formatting you want and you cursor will then turn into the Border Painter paint brush and all of your color, width, and style settings will adjust to match the line you sampled from.

From there you can then apply that formatting using any of the options we discussed above.

Be careful with this one because the first line you click on will be sampled and any line after that will take the formatting of the first line. I messed this up a few times by clicking on one line and then another expecting the second click to take that second line's formatting until I remembered enough to not do that.

If you sample from the wrong line the first time, use Esc to turn the Border Painter off and then try again.

Text Direction

By default, the text in the cells in a table will be aligned just like normal text and will run from left to right across the cell. You can change the text direction, however, so that the text runs up and down.

The best way to see the available options is to right-click on your table and choose Text Direction from the dropdown menu.

This will bring up the Text Direction - Table Cell dialogue box.

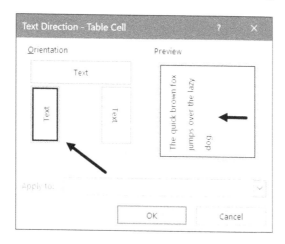

The left-hand side of the dialogue box shows the three available orientation options. The right-hand side shows a preview of the currently-selected option.

To apply a text direction, select the cells in your table, right-click, choose Text Direction, click on the direction you want, and then click on OK.

You can also use the Text Direction option in the Alignment section of the Table Tools Layout tab. Clicking on it will change the direction of the text in your selected cells. Each time you click on it, the text in your table will rotate to the next option. (There is no dropdown so you have to rotate through.)

Text Alignment

In addition to the direction of the text, you can also change the alignment of the text. Alignment works along two dimensions. One of the dimensions is top, center, or bottom. The other dimension is left, center, or right.

Combine the two and you get nine choices. For example, Top Left, Top Center, and Top Right for the three top of a cell alignment choices.

You can left, center, or right-align text in a table using the Paragraph section of the Home tab,. Control shortcuts (Ctrl + E, R, and L) will also work for center, right, and left alignment if you're working with a subset of the cells in a table.

But the only place to also assign top, middle or bottom placement of your text is in the Alignment section of the Table Tools Layout tab. There you can see visual representations of each choice and simply click on the one you want to apply to your selected cells

Here are examples of all nine choices applied to cells in a table:

Top Left	Top Center	Top Right
Center Left	Center	Center Right
Bottom Left	Bottom Center	Bottom Right

Spacing Between Cells

You can also format a table so that there are spaces between each of the cells in the table. To do so, click on your table, go to the Alignment section of the Table Tools Layout tab, and click on Cell Margins

This will bring up the Table Options dialogue box. If you click on Allow Spacing Between Cells and specify a value that will place a space between each cell in your table. If you use a visible border line on the interior of your table each cell will have its own border and then there will be white space between all of the cells.

You can also bring up the Table Options dialogue box by right-clicking on your table, choosing Table Properties from the dropdown menu, and then clicking on Options from the Table tab.

Other

My personal preference is to do all calculations, sorting, and data analysis in Excel and then just copy the results into Word when I'm done. However, Word does allow for some manipulation of your data within a table. (Aside from the embedded Excel file option we discussed earlier that kept crashing on me.)

So I'm going to cover these options here, but this is not how I recommend doing this.

Sorting

You can actually sort lines of text in Word without having them in a table. For example, you could have a list of five words in Word, each on a separate line, and have Word sort them by using the A to Z option in the Paragraph section of the Home tab.

It's far more likely, though, that you'd want to Sort entries in a table.

For example, if I decide to use Word to keep track of all of the books I've read in a year. I'm just going to enter them in my table one-by-one. But come the end of the year I might decide I want that list to be alphabetical by title or author rather than sorted by date.

To sort the entries in a table, select the whole table (by clicking the little square with four arrows in the top left corner), go to the Table Tools Layout tab and click on the Sort option in the Data section on the right-hand side. (It has a big stacked AZ with an arrow.)

This will bring up the Sort dialogue box.

If you have a header row in your table, tell Word and it will label your options using the labels in your header row. Otherwise it will just number the columns.

(The option to say you have a header row is at the bottom of the dialogue box not the top like it is in Excel.)

You can then choose to sort your table by the values in up to three different columns. The first column you list will be the main one used in the sort. The second listed column will only be used if two rows have the same value for the first column. Same for the third, it will only be used if the values in the first AND second column are the same for at least two entries.

For each column you can choose to sort in either ascending or descending order and you can specify to Word whether the contents of the cells should be treated as text, numbers, or dates. (Word will try to make that assignment itself, but you can change it.)

Once you've made your selections click on OK.

Formulas

Word does have a formula option in the Table Tools Layout tab but you'll need to know a bit about formulas in Excel to use it effectively. It also appears to only work on one cell at a time.

To use this option, click into a cell in your table and then go to the Table Tools Layout tab and click on Formula. This will bring up a Formula dialogue box.

Word may suggest a formula to you based on the contents of the table, but it also may not. If it doesn't, you can go down to the Paste function option at the bottom of the dialogue box and choose from the list of functions in the dropdown menu. (The Help text for this option lists out what each function can do.)

Choosing to paste a function will paste an empty version of that function into the Formula line. You'll then need be able to complete it yourself.

The basic use of formulas in Word relies on using the positional arguments, LEFT, RIGHT, ABOVE, and BELOW.

For example,

$$=SUM(LEFT)$$

will sum all numbers in the cells in that row that are to the left of the cell you're in.

$$=AVERAGE(ABOVE)$$

will average the numbers in the cells in the same column that are above the cell.

$$=PRODUCT(RIGHT)$$

will take the product of the values in the cells in that row that are to the right of the current cell.

You can combine two of the positional arguments, so:

$$=SUM(LEFT,ABOVE)$$

will sum all cells in that row to the left and all cells in that column that are above the cell with the formula.

After you've placed a formula in your table, select the table and use F9 to update the formula. Otherwise the value in your formula will not reflect the current value. You can also just highlight the value in that one cell and use F9.

Be careful with text values in your cell range. They may not behave as expected in your formula.

If you don't want to use the positional arguments, you can also use A1 notation which is how you reference a cell in Excel. So Cell A1 is in the first column and first row. Cell C3 is in the third column and third row.

To specify the format of your result, use the Number format dropdown choices in the dialogue box.

(Unfortunately, those number formats are only available for when you use a formula, so if you have fixed numeric values that you want formatted in a specific way you need to format those in Excel and then copy them into Word or manually create the appearance of the format you want for each cell.)

Convert to Text

There have been times when I copied information into Word and it copied in as a table but I didn't want it to be a table

The way to fix this is to select the table, go to the Data section of the Table Tools Layout tab, and click on Convert to Text.

A Convert Table to Text dialogue box will appear that lets you choose how to separate each entry. You can choose paragraph marks, tabs, commas, or your own separator. Once done, click OK.

The text will no longer be in a table, but the values from the table will still be in your document.

If you use paragraph marks each entry from the table will appear on its own line. If you use a different separator option, values for each row of the table will appear on a line together with each column's values separated by your chosen separator.

(Sometimes when I do this I need everything listed together in a simple paragraph with each enttry separated by a comma. To get that result I combine Convert to Text with Find and Replace to change the line break for each row to a comma and a space.)

Conclusion

Alright, so that was the basics of tables in Word 2019. If you get stuck, reach out and I'm happy to help if I can. I don't check email every day, but I do check it regularly.

Good luck with it.

And if you decide that you want to learn more about Microsoft Word or Word 2019, feel free to check out my other books.

Appendix A: Basic Terminology

Below are some basic terms that I use throughout this guide.

Tab

I refer to the menu choices at the top of the screen (File, Home, Insert, Design, Layout, References, Mailings, Review, View, and Help) as tabs.

Click

If I tell you to click on something, that means to use your mouse (or trackpad) to move the arrow on the screen over to a specific location and left-click or right-click on the option. If I don't specify which to use, left-click.

Select or Highlight

If I tell you to select text, that means to highlight that text either by using your mouse or the arrow and shift keys. Selected text is highlighted in gray.

Dropdown Menu

A dropdown menu provides you a list of choices to select from. There are dropdown menus when you right-click in your document workspace as well as for some of the options listed under the tabs at the top of the screen. Each option with a small arrow next to it will have a dropdown menu available.

Expansion Arrows

I refer to the little arrows at the bottom right corner of most of the sections in each tab as expansion arrows. For example, click on the expansion arrow in the Clipboard section of the Home tab and it will open the Clipboard task pane.

Dialogue Box

Dialogue boxes are pop-up boxes that cover specialized settings. They allow the most granular level of control over an option.

Scroll Bar

Scroll bars are on the right-hand side of the workspace and sometimes along the bottom. They allow you to scroll through your document if your text takes up more space than you can see in the workspace.

Arrow

If I ever tell you to arrow to the left or right or up or down, that just means use your arrow keys.

Task Pane

I refer to the panes that sometimes appear to the left, right, and bottom of the main workspace as task panes. By default you should see the Navigation task pane on the left-hand side when you open a new document in Word.

Control Shortcut

I'll occasionally mention control shortcuts that you can use to perform tasks. When I reference them I'll do so by writing it as Ctrl + a capital letter. For example, Save is Ctrl + S.

To use one, hold down the Ctrl key and the letter at the same time.

ABOUT THE AUTHOR

M.L. Humphrey is a former stockbroker with a degree in Economics from Stanford and an MBA from Wharton who has spent close to twenty years as a regulator and consultant in the financial services industry.

You can reach M.L. Humphrey at:

mlhumphreywriter@gmail.com

or at

www.mlhumphrey.com

www.ingramcontent.com/pod-product-compliance
Lightning Source LLC
Chambersburg PA
CBHW060508060326
40689CB00020B/4682